Cross Connections

Renuka Raghavan

BookLeaf
Publishing

India | USA | UK

Presentation by *BookLeaf Publishing*

Web: www.bookleafpub.com

E-mail: info@bookleafpub.com

ISBN:9789363317956

First edition 2024

To

Arjun and Abhirami

ACKNOWLEDGEMENT

Many thanks to BookLeaf Publishing for all their support and primarily for having ignited the spark in me to restart writing.

PREFACE

Cross-Connections is my attempt at sketching short snippets from life in the form of poems.

This collection was born after the heartwarming response I received for my first book, 'Musings in Random Order', published in December 2023.

Many of my poems have our little daughter Ami peeping out of them, as she is terribly missed after being with us for a mere fifteen months before having gone forever.

Subtle Reminders

What is it that reminds me of you?
Is it the diaper that sits on the rack?

Or is it the twinkle in the kitten's eye?
Is it the voice of the little girl next door ?

Or is it the scent of the rose that just bloomed?
Is it the soft hair of the baby in that pram?

Or is it the moon that comes out all calm?
Is it the warmest sweater that hangs in the
closet?

Or is it the song that plays on the car radio?
Is it the Barbie that I see over the counter?
Or is it the summer ray that shimmers through ?

Well maybe?

Is it the cut off edges of your passport that I
treasure?
Or is it the cold tap water that runs down
my back?

Is it the saddening siren of the ambulance that
rushes?
Or is it the still air that fills the elevator?

There's no reminder good enough I'd vouch
Than the very air I breathe... in and out

Without a pause, without a break
You visit me daily my precious one

In moments of joy and sorrow alike
Holding me tight and just alright..

Tucking her in

He planted some love
In those tall glass bottles
That once stored her favourite
Fruity Chardonnay wine

He placed a few red walnuts
In the glass bowl on the table
Particularly choosing them
As she would like them not bitter

He placed the T.V remote
Right above the books on the shelf
Carefully pushing them in
Lest they would fall, as she would do

He arranged his cluttered wardrobe
Folding away those tees
Neatly stacking one over the other
Quite like her, humming a favorite tune

He cleaned the white China ware
With the liquid by the sink
Just a dip and a scrub
Even hearing her say, that will do, not more

He walked back to push the coir mat
Edging the door corners
As though measuring the gaps
To avoid a side jut, like she would do

He went about with life
Not giving into his grief
Of having lost his soul mate
His twin flame, his friend

Tucking her in...
Within the warmth of the soft cushions
Resting on their sofa
Where she would curl up, reading a book

The wooden box in the corner

It was long since she had opened the wooden
box
That sat frozen in time, in the corner of her room

She heard its hinges creak in pain
As she lifted the heavy lid to rest it against the
wall

She heard the drums of her beating heart
As she held back the avalanche of emotions

The red kancheevaram sari bordered with gold
zari
The off white dawani that exuded elegance

The heavy anklets wrapped in soft muslin
Clinking swollen cries of joy on being nudged

The huge kadas of gold that lazily lay on their
cotton beds
Not losing their sheen even after the many years
that passed

She quietly picked up the heavy lump
That sat softly wrapped in the old napkin

She heard a melancholy in the background
That echoed her tune, sad and cracked

The jhumkas were big and bright in gold
Bringing back his memories, bold

She mothered them with hands so soft
And hugged them in an embrace warm

Just then the wall clock ticked a 12 noon
Causing her to spring up with the lump

In her palms and her throat...
The stones were a striking red and green

Secured tightly with the sparkling diamond

She tilted her head to her left
As she wore the jhumka

Promptly twisting the screw at the back
She secured her thoughts tight and neat

Deciding to be happy, in total control
Deliberately ignoring the trickle of the tear......

Living the remains

The breeze played quietly
With her fine brown hair
Opening loose strands over her face
Caressing her subtly painted lips...

Parting her lips
Breaking open a faint smile
Her breath rhythmic but heavy
Left her chest rise up and down in waves

Her eyes loosely sealed
Fluttering long lashes
Not giving away slightest hints
Of where her thoughts wandered

Her tender but pounding heart
Felt swollen and stollen
She felt his presence in the air around
That engulfed her in softening hugs

Her legs curled up in comfort poses
Bringing herself to secret reminders
Of aching joys and scented hugs
That brought with it subtle emotions

Her pillows whispered a secret tale
Of the night that passed, in quiet echoes
Soaking her within, an ocean of madness
That left her rise and sink in delight.

Slow Mornings

She tossed and turned in bed today
Waiting to see if she could sleep some more
Having chosen a 'work from home'
She deliberately delayed the alarm

Taking a slow shower in the morning
Was a luxury far from possible
As she left for work at seven sharp
Not affording to miss a minute

The colorless dollop popped out
As she pumped the bottle soft
Her coconut husk lathered smooth
Along her gentle shoulders

Wrapped in a soft dry towel
She walked across the room
The eucalyptus scent lingered
As she sat to dry her hair

A white kurta, starched and pressed
Was what she chose to wear
And no perfume would be sprayed
As she wanted to breathe the air

She measured the coffee powder
Spooning it out of the tin
Allowing herself to sniff it nice
And tapping it on the sides

Standing on her dainty toes
She reached out for the strings
And drew open the light blue curtains
To let the warm lights in

Further pushing open the windows
She hooked the stoppers to their holes
What delight it was she thought
To embrace the morning sun....

Close Encounter

The dog's bark got me racing
With fast approaching footsteps
The crickets had joined the race
Deciding to screech along

My heart beats sounded louder
And anklet tinkled clearer
Not thinking twice
I sprinted with all my might

The steel spoon clattered along
Inside the empty steel dabba
In my bright yellow tote bag
That I gathered with both my hands

The roads narrowed as I turned
The street lights dimmed as I hurried
The trees creaked in the wind
Where the owls hooted in gaps

I heard the persistent cycle bell
That followed me vigorously
My steps now grew even larger
And I gasped for a whiff of breath

There were broken glasses below
That were swept aside neatly
The touch-me-nots grinned wickedly
Until I victoriously brushed them aside

I tripped over a careless branch
That had fallen from the mango tree
Not knowing how to pounce back up
And set off on a quick escape

My feet were caught rather hurriedly
As though I'd slither away
Like a snake that found its hole
Where its eggs lay quiet and careful

I dared not turn and look back
At the horrid face behind me
I held tight with all my might
To the gate right in front of me

You'll be late for school today
Was what I heard the next
Sweating rather profusely
I was awakened by my mother

Glad I wasn't simply living
The dream I saw until then
I quickly got up and ran
To check if I was hurt...

Loud whispers

The paper plate struggled to stay
As Abrar held it with his hand
The wind was harsh today
Not knowing it was his only meal

A cup of yoghurt
A dry round kuboose
He soaked each bit carefully
And chewed with all his might

His hunger seemed satiated
As he gulped down the food
Hoping he'd get an overtime tonight
Letting him stay back at the warehouse

His room would be crammed
As visitors come to stay
It was the weekend tonight
But Abrar found it hard

To enjoy the deafening company
Of the nine and plus people
Who would come over to make merry
In their small and dingy room

Life in the opulent desert city
Was busy and loud like no other
But deep within the many noises
Was the quiet of Abrar's mind

He missed his lady back home
Who waited for his messages
And ammi who earnestly prayed
For his health and long life

His ten-sharing tiny room
Felt like heaven at night
When he sank into his bunk bed
And fell unconscious in a blink

Today wasn't his best
As he yearned for peace and quiet
And not the chattering company
Of all the nine who'd come

Hues of unison

Her eyes mildly flickered
As she watched the long train
That chugged off the tracks
In paints of red and yellow

She sat quietly in the halted rickshaw
A green, yellow and black
As it puffed and panted in measured gaps
Patiently waiting at the railway crossing

She faintly smiled at herself in awe
As it amused her quite child-like
That she too wore a pretty Bengal sari
That was another bright yellow and red

The sari, starched to perfection
The rickshaw, freshly coated

The train, stained from seasons battered
But all carrying their colours proudly

Seemingly strange as she paused to notice
That they were sketches in some artist's larger
canvas
The three of them in matching loud hues
For any particular reason, she knew not though...

Peeping Back

As she walked through the corridors
She met the little girl from the past
The navy blue pinafore over a white collared
shirt
Blue socks and buckled black shoes

The loosely braided hair
Neat and fresh after wash
Dried up sandalwood paste
On her wide-broad forehead

Her kajal drawn bright eyes
Winged like a cat on the sides
A steel dabba in the sling bag
With a hot meal for lunch break

Pictures from the forgotten past
And scenes flashed before her eyes
Like the trailer of a newly released movie
But with no suspense to wait for

Other than a few memories
And pumped up nostalgia
Coated with worldly wisdom
In gallons of love and affection
She sat near the open windows
With wind in her hair
Entangling the loose strands
Crafting a careless picture

The master noticed her stillness
Which he found rather uncanny
He sensed some sober mischief
Brimming in the back seat

He called aloud her name
To which she bounced upright
Staring at the master
Who stared back annoyed

I quickly set off to the staff room
To check if master was there
He sat quietly lost in thoughts
Next to the many bundle of books

Munching on the remains of a toffee
Possibly shared by a birthday boy
I went upto him pausing a bit
To see if I would be welcomed at all

His forehead gathered a few fine lines
Trying to recollect who I was
93 batch, 10 A sir
Oh isn't that you, my naughty little girl?

The lady behind the veil

She saw the crowd
Through her veil
Screaming abuses
Loud and clear

There were hundreds
Assembled there
Both men and women
And children too

Their screams fell loud
On her ears
And deep within
They left her hollow

She gasped for breath
As she waded through
They pushed and pulled
And went frantic altogether

The rare times ever
That she possibly looked up
She saw them stare
And throw curses many

They came right straight
And entered her deep
As though arrows sharp
That came shooting at her

But once she bowed
And waded through
Their screams had faded
And lost their force

She heard none now
Not the faintest scream
But echoes within
Left her heart to bleed

The silence was deafening
And chewed her senses
As she climbed the steps
Of the tall police jeep

Kurinji poocha

Kurinji was a cotton ball
She had eyes like bulbs
Amber yellow insides
With vertical pupils, barely a line

She closed them tight
As she meowed quite soft
Purring in between
Her secret weapon

She sat close pawed
Circling her tail in
Outlining her proud stance
Displaying a queenly poise

Kurinji had come home
With no invitation
She walked in one evening
With eyes that twinkled

Black patches here and there
Scattered over her white coat
Like pieces of a jigsaw puzzle
That fitted out of place

Kurinji had a fluffy tail
More like a bushy broom
That she used in her favour
Time and again

Kurinji would not be tamed
As she was her own master
She left every night
Eyes glowing in the dark

Drab life

The stain on his teeth
Were a rusty red
That gave hints
Of his rugged mind

His steady stare
Was a sight of fright
That could bring to dust
The mortal in focus

His mundu was a brown
With patches of mud
Gathered at the waist
Quite careless and untidy

His gait was limpy
But momentum quite speedy
As though he was in a hurry
To find something he'd lost

His house was a one room
Thatched with leaves
Come summer or rain
It sheltered him fine

The walls had scratches
From the years of living
The floors had deep cracks
From feet that were heavy

Life rarely happened
Within those four walls
Though years had passed
Living life all alone

A quiet evening

The sky turned a faint orange
As the day drew closer to dusk
Her face lit up a pretty pink
As she sat immersed in thoughts

The road ahead lay barren and still
With not much movement in sight
The lamps glowed a light yellow hue
Casting shaped shades beneath them

Her forehead gathered pensive lines
As she gazed at the stars above
Her thoughts had stocked up right and left
Quite neatly in a handsome pile

The clouds had hidden themselves today
As though not wanting to be found astray
They led way for a clear neat sky
For stars to line up quiet

They gazed at us from right above
Reminding us that they were there
Not forgetting things, not fading away
Stealthily shining through tinkling eyes

Feeling you

Today again, I took you in my hands
Felt your little forehead that was hurt
From the fall you had from the chair
When I was cleaning the pantry shelf

I noticed your soft brown hair
Loosely falling over your eyes
It had a lustrous shine to it
With a tint of golden hue too

The tinkle in your eyes were there
Sparkling through as I held you close
And how your smile curved at your lip
Just enough to make me happy

The flush of pink on your cheeks
Once again I looked for them
They simply plumped them even round
Tiny plums, they had ripened well

My lips pressed close on yours, again
When I felt torn and battered within
As it had dawned that you were gone
And what I held was just a frame

How everytime I dust the shelf
I need to stop and carry you once
Look at you and smile at you
Plant a kiss and wipe a tear

Uphill

The bus puffed up the hilly road
Winding slow and pulling hard
The climb was steep and scary too
We sat intact holding tight onto bars in front

As we went high up , I looked beneath
The valley down was green and neat
The houses seemed like biscuits lined
In many rows , neatly layered

The cars and buses seemed little too
They looked like those from 'Hot Wheels' sets
The trees were pointed to the sky
Standing tall and aiming high

The temples , churches and mosques were there
They looked quite calm and content within
With flowers strewn over and blanketed in mist

Nature had a way of taming men
Pricking bloated pride and loud sermons

Rain

As he started his car
He was still thinking of work
The laptop emitted heat today
The day was long and tiring too

The skies looked dark and cloudy now
Just then he remembered the weather warning
The signal took long as usual there
Which means he'd get the next one too

It had started to rain by then
Light drizzles , it may subside
But as he drove a good ride ahead
It started pouring and how hard now

The wipers tried hard to swipe them away
But the waters turned aggressive soon
They fell with vengeance from above

As though a leak had burst open wide

The thunders came soon in roaring might
Causing him to fret and panic
Agony and pain had bundled up into one
Making all to run and hide

The journey was treacherous to say the least
But he had to get home sooner now
To check if they were safe and sound
Within the walls of their humble home

The rains poured harder and storms grew harsher
Every person rang a distress bell
Knowing not how to pass the misery
Of having been stuck on road all way

Home coming

As she looked through the window
She saw the shabby white taxi
Driving away , the tail lights fading
Into the tall trees that stood on sides

Her wait for the great holiday
And the excitement the wait brought..
Everything was done with now
As the car motored away ...

Every year it came and went
For 10 years in total now...
The details of prepping the house
To welcome her special boy

He was not a child anymore
But he was hers after all
Growing big made no difference
He was her little boy , big and strong!

Lone and alone

She held one side and routed the other
Securing the end onto the hook
The tiny bells tinkled ever so softly
As they exchanged sombre secrets

Her long fingers ran over them
In a bid to hush them quiet
She examined her toe nails, just incase
They needed a filing to keep their shine

The anklets wrapped her feet in elegance
As she tip-toed across the room
She broke the silence that hovered around
For she was all alone...

Her glass bangles , red and white
Were pretty with dots sprinkled over
She brushed them inside to hear them tinkle
With polished fingers long and neat

Her necklace was an antique kundan
Green and white and red pressed
Loosely hugging her lean long neck
As though securing her collars

Loving herself was a mastered art
Whenever she felt blue and low
She knew she had to pump herself up
As there was no one ...she was all alone..

The decision

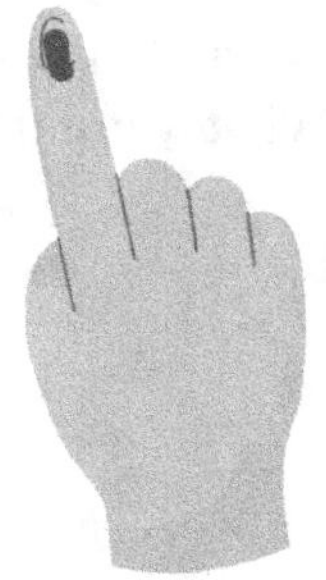

The photograph matched
The name, spotted and circled
Read aloud for someone to note
The finger was inked and I was in

Names, photographs , symbols, parties
Everything went hayway in my mind
I glanced at the list on the white board
It was long, a colourless list it appeared

The buttons on the sides staring at me
Waiting to be pressed at my free will
What could possibly my lone vote do?
But I want to decide, when given a chance!

Later I cannot fret and complain aloud
That oh what a guy! Who elected him?
I had a chance to get him out
And I sat at home fearing the heat

Opinions matter everywhere
Casting your vote is a right
Never to be missed
Whatever it takes.

Holding on

Like a droplet that balanced over
The wide grin of the Colocasia

The rainbow that strained itself
To be break open across the morning sky

Like the ripest mango on the light branch
That held on for life with all its might

The candle wick that kept its dying flame
As the wind blew hard through the door

The little girl on the shore standing firm
As the sand pulled away from beneath

Life is but a battle of might
That we ferociously fight
As the world watches
In stealth and in silence

Does it matter?

Does it matter if I wore a black bindi?
Or does it matter if I left it bare between my
eyes?
Maybe a medium sized red bindi will do....

Does it matter if I applied an eye shadow?
Or does it matter if I winged my eyes?
Maybe 'simple' kajal lined eyes will do...

Does it matter if I wore lipstick?
Or does it matter if I wore a lip gloss?
Maybe a nude balm will do...

Does it matter if I left my neck bare?
Or does it matter if I wore a collared blouse?
Maybe a fine gold necklace will do...
Does it matter if I wore a sleeveless?

Or does it matter if I wore a half sleeve?
Maybe showing no skin will do...

Does it matter if I went for a girls' night out?
Or does it matter if I went to a friend's place for
dinner?
Maybe having a day out will do....

When what you do
Does not matter to you
But does matter to them,
You are introduced to a new person
The "you" that you "ought to be"...